The

Open

*poetry
of a
divine union
with
The Beloved*

Sara Laya Heartloom

The Blossom Opens to Open

poetry
of a
divine union
with
The Beloved

Sara Laya Heartloom

ISBN-13: 978-1519497239
ISBN-10: 1519497237

This heart is so alive.
The revelation is in
the love making,
making
Us.

Create.
I tremble and soar when
I create you creating me.

~

The Divine makes Itself known
in the heat of the subtle dance
of inner union
felt in musical
and artistic creation.

Words storming,
colors whirling,
and voice soaring,
I am most in Love,
when creating.

Dedicated to,
My Beloved, the Great Friend:
the Ever Present One.

~ < > ~

I offer my gratitude to beloved Binah May Zing, who taught me the loving no; my cohort of cosmic love: 'Campamocha'; sisters of Blue Mountain; the Sol Nectar sisters; my Peruvian medicine family of Wiracocha; the Fisher brothers; my heart-warrior-ally, Bee; my dear friend, Niko, and...the guardian spirits of 'Shatara.'

Gratitude and love to all my ancestral family; Mary Brinkley and Rick Allen, and Rebekah J.,Grandma Jean, my aunt, Kathleen, and so many more.

Introduction

This collection of poems was written over the short span of one summer spent living in the woods, on a lush piece of Oregon land I refer to as 'Shatara.' Nestled into a meadow, in a large tent, I retreated. I decided to step away from an 11-year kundalini yoga practice, following a spontaneous 'awakening', as I sat in the basement of an athletic club in downtown Portland. Keeping in mind that placing any word upon these transcendent experiences is like trying to maneuver the oceans of the world into one fish bowl, I will attempt to extrapolate: I was having a break between two classes I taught, sitting and breathing. The next moment, my mind plummeted downward, my awareness rooted in my belly and body. My womb and belly pulsed in an easeful rhythm to the infinite potential of the momentary spaciousness. All directions came at me, as I gave my breath unto them. Merging with the essence of life, umbilicus cord to Source, my body intelligence spoke, "there is no turning around, now. The shedding of skins is only just beginning"

In the months to follow, in meditation, I would sweat many a morning, from the blazing heat beating on my tent.. The steam of that which I purged would leak into sweat, tears, and these woven words.

In essence, this is a journey of healing from a life of violence, abuse, and sexual violation. It is the story of the trespassed Womb, of which millions of women will relate to. It tells of coming home, in victory and self-forgiveness. It tells of going through the rage and shame, leading to making peace with the past. It is the story of an electrified romance – internal and external - and the alchemy of music. It tells of healing distrust of the masculine and honoring sexuality as sacred. Finally, it is the most blazing Love story of my life, inspired by the inner marriage of anima and animus, muse and musician.

May these words inspire others to open their own hearts and voices to the shadows they have lived through, for the highest good of us all.

6

Contents

The Birth

The Life

The Death

The Union

~ the birth

~Loosening The Hook

There is a fascist sex goddess
within me.
I stare at her in awe and fear.

What if
What if?
My fear of her is no more than
 my
Desire to be her?

I merge with the one
who seeks to control.
(I face her)

Enter her womb,
I breathe with her.

Around her gleaming jewels,
I kiss her bare skin.

I will not be blinded by
The shine of her silver.

I will dare to meet her gaze
And then... let the stars witness us.

She will loosen her garments.
She will let her gems fall away.

Revealing the original pristine
Shine of her shores and seas.

Witnessing us
as
power meets fear
and melds into pleasure,
Awe,
and wonder.

The child is conceived.
Star -baby breathes
Life into
 life
Into life.

~Celebration

The table is made.
I set down my cup.
And allow God to celebrate
seeing you.
Seeing me.

Our medicine is sweet
...and jolting.

The table
Is the dancing floor.
I pocket my No.

Divulge my Yes and More,
As a maiden with feathers
I made in the dark weather
When my heart folded
Unto itself
To learn
The sutra of self
Loving self
Loving..
 self Loving..
 self.

These hands are hot
and tremble
In yours.
Brandishing feathers,
I made in the cold weather,

as if they could hold
all.
this.
love.
I trust
in their
desire to fly
and
instinct to stand by.

                they can carry Love
                alchemizing into this,
                this breath exchange.
                Interchange.
                base metals to Gold.
                key in keyhole.

How can I say no?

~Void

Enamored silence.
I am ready now
For your medicine.

And you remind me
Its not that important.
But let's not relinquish words
From a poet.

Still -
You prescribe light
with a lightness of being.

Then light reaches so deep,
 I forget momentarily
The light you wish to teach.
 because -
Love loves to be made in the dark,
in the corridor of hot winds and waters.
I arouse form into more form
until
 light hits my body

I see patterns fruit from lush mind.

Until
All
fruit
falls.

heavy in the burgeoning light.

So . . . the void
Is dark arousing light.
The whirring quiver
The weaver and weaving
Laughing at each other.

~Vapor

The true art of desire:
  know less..
  feel more.

Be in the heart of the knowing.
 folding and unfolding.
Peer into
 the window-panes of pristine trust.
Nestle into
 the blankets of divine laziness.

mind
offer waters
 for
the flora
 soul gathers
and
 heart sings.

Even this,
Is tenuous.
These words are
 vapor –

distilling.

the
  essence has
    the sweetest taste.

~I am it

Home.
Coming home.
I'm gathering in.
Tender and loving.
Nothing missing.
For nothing is sought.

Twinkle in eyes
Wrinkle in smile.

You ask me to be with who?

'Myself,' I reply, with resolve.

When I yearn
And the seeking returns –
Can this music be enough?
Can our melodies make love?

the stars emit light
and kiss the borders of night

I am it.

~Part of the Way

What is it?
What am I?

I contract when I attach to knowing you.
I would grapple for more answers –
Or –
I can fall away and let it all fall.
Move out the way and be of it all.

(if its in the way,
    it's part of the way,
        it's okay)

Sovereign self
This is the most afraid I've ever been.
And the truth moves my marrow.
Of this choice (choosing me)
 to be alone.

These tears move from despair
To the warm reunion: I'm here.

I spoke to you last night
Over rose tea
I said that I wish could be ready.
I desired to be where I was not–
to be with you.
There is a union my soul signals from.
Therein hides the paradox.
My desire to be with you is

my desire to be with me.
I desire to be where I am –
  to be with you.
I am where I am,
  you are the being as much as
I am.

Wait!
I turn in again.
I turn in to my heart.

I turn in to me.
I turn in to me.

I hear -
you,
  singing river.
You sing aside me.
Our voices make love.
It's part of the way.

I fall away,
The song is the water, the ripples and sea
Where I offer my weight.
and all that I think.

The stories drift endlessly.
I am a weightless weaver,
Even a non-believer.

Absorbed beyond words - in vibration.
I like this play,
Flying each story out to the winds.
No more carrying.
I am a naked child, giggling,
Tossing her toys over the cliff.
I know,

I know nothing.

~ the life

~Empty Room Full Womb

Virgin soul
Beckoning me home.
No more I forsake the gifts
 that must be given.
Herein lies my power
 and our medicine.
Within my sacred cistern.
Sacred sisters and child.
Breathing from the cauldron
Of life.
I had to burn, cremate primate mind
Yes, I did die.
Another phoenix doth arise.
Blown to the wind, scattered stories.
Resurrect
 pure essence.

Resurr~Essence.

Sovereign soul,
Man of light.
Light choosing man.
I won't blow this out of proportion –

    I   feel   your   Samadhi.
    Your   love   blowing   open....

Pristine glow through your eyes and skin.
I recognize beauty.

God within.
All within.

Flames are twin.
That story becomes vapor.
as definition ceases to matter.
Matter alchemizes to light.
We return to electric synergy,
 the challenge to evolve.
Fire balls and playful energy.
Relationship shifts, a ship on the sea.
Let the waters carry it, craft it to be what it will be.

There was a dis-ease in me.
Life –sucking entity.
I realized the drain and that power of demand.
I thank you, human~mirrors, who have taught me.
Light beings, reminding me of light - - I Am Being.

Process no more with you
Not with force will I spill on you
I surrender control so we might
 reconcile fire and light.
Combat and build each other up,
instead of fight to wear each other down.

I love this new paradigm.
Music,
water on fire,
electric chemistry.

My lover and mate is now
 this 3d reality.
I am fully here.
Incarnate and of the earth.
Earth into rebirth.
RebEarth.

Curious about the relationship
....with
....with...
   what I love.

I love.

I will build my nest and tea house.
Crystal beings, sage, and sauerkraut.
Dawn, step on her grass,
  Sing with bird coos.
Dusk, hear stars whisper oracles,
  Alight star seeds in my womb.

~ Voice Loom

Weave worlds with your words.
Word and world,
One in the same
Same in the One.
Voice open,
Stretch, textiles soften.
Fibers of silk,
 long forgotten,
Longing to be touched
By your warm wind –

Ear to chest and breath,
 Listen to the silent sounds.
Those seeds not watered - yet.

  I sing

to you
what I hear
in you.

I may secure your loom frame
til your heart pumps,
ready to weave again.

Then -

oh.

Then -

Lean in close
and feel the medicine of
  you.
Your song,
  your sounds,
    and your silence.

Sing and speak truth.
Speak and sing it through.
because the world
prays to weave words through you.
and words pray to weave worlds for you.

~Still, I am It

I feel ready for a God incarnate.
My Shiva in mirrored armor.
Revealing my folds and golden skin.
He can go through it all with me.

Or can he? Will he?
What is the true need?

All that I once knew...

dissolves.
Now tender and soft,
I make love to my gold.
Open and pliant,
Gleaming shine.

I am it.
I am it.

I am...

This medicine,

Yours,

Is my own.
Not ours to own, own, own

Your mirror is pure.
Waters disrupted
the reflection is corrupted

maintain a still lake.
Allow the music to ripple the weight.

Channel pain into beauty.
Face it.
Its been the art of humanity
For infinite centuries.

Health and healing

Creation and creating.

Life giving unto life
Make art of our deaths.

Another phoenix doth arise
Ashes to song and color lines.

I live to create,
The womb is not mine alone.
Empty room equals full womb.
Voices of the ages,
Birth through me.
A woman fertile with star seeds,
I am bringing life through labor pains
Of a life fully lived,
Of the wounds fully felt,
This life is art,
This life is art,
A temple space realizing
Greif and thousands of tastes
Becoming sweet
and sweeter
Through
voice and color.
Everywhere I am,
I am the mother.
The lover and daughter,
and..
The king, my playful mate
He and I cannot help but to create.

Create. Create.
Cremate with electric zing
That which is the offering.
That which once was felt as pain.
Electric nectar now sweetens the game.

Evolve and expand.
Stretch the solar plexus into our hands.

feel
ascend,
 release.
repeat.

feel
ascend,
 release.
repeat.

and begin,
and begin
 again...

~Play Alone

This aloneness.
All one ness.
I love this.
My laughter peals out
 on wings,
flys back into me.
Sings ripples
back through me.
All for me.
This spaciousness
 is
  selfishness
becoming
  self-Us-ness.

Dare say..
   self-less-ness.

Absorption and play.
Hurling self over precipice
Yes, I will get used to this -
this getting used to me.
Used and loose.
Unfettered, unfurled.
Gathering in to tend.
Tenderness.
This all-one-ness.
  bliss alone,
  this.

~Caramel Space Drip

Let it be
Lay ah lay ah
Let it be

'Cause the space
it tastes so sweet.

the space tastes
like candy
my mind melts
like caramel
and lets it drip
it all drips down
through it all
through me
through it all

through me

through less structure
stability
comes
from the ground...less space
where the roots want to give way
where they want to grow and play
our music can make love
and our words weave worlds
and music weaves worlds into us.

Making reality our being
Reality evolving
Evolving through
this play this space
Create creation
Then..

~Sha-Sister Medicine Again

feeling raw
from numb,
defrost
the fear
in my chest
and let the weeping
wetness
wash.

Star wash
full moon

birds songs
a morning coo

I arise again
wishing to speak with you,
then she says recall the "king"
I wanted you to meet?

Magic maker
sister of mine,
How did you know?
You saw our flame shine?

Before we met
In physical presence
Our music made love
in an intuitive sense.

I request to
Breathe around this
To let it fly again
Weightless I am.
Wait for this, I can.

Emotions felt
With tenderness
My hands, his hands.
Attention given.

That's my cultivation
Feel and expand
Expansive field
Hold her hand.

Through it all:
Expansion does not mean
Abandon.

Feeling is felt into streams
   of colors and
Sound waves
Silent sound rays
Breath game,
   radiant play.

~Madness Openness Sadness Joy

Like never before
I catalyze the emotions
Forest fire anger,
Into ornate poetry.
Release the liver
Cleanse with water
Weeping water
   word weavings.

I have a teacher
She asks me to feel
and opens the space
To make love to this
Life lived mystery,
   to feel into word weavings
   without analytical thinking.

She is an ancient grandma
Teaching me the art of cackle
The tools of healthy silence
   and kitchen listening.

She asks me to be water
To keep moving over stone

To trust their solidarity
Is to trust my fluid strength.

Its solid structure never lost
Only softened over time, time felt.
The earth holds us,
Water babies, remembering, we melt.

Ripple and drip
Through the dense stability
Celebrate in
her inherent
Holding,
so we may let go.

So we may let fall.

~**Little Pear**

Now.
This is a new story
Old ones washed clean,
on down the stream..

Sweet pear
Poised on your stem
Internal
Inherent erection
Sovereign
Safe, full, and alive.

What will we carry now?
You and I..

31

There is so much life
To fertilize.

I love you,
Little pear of mine.

~Listening

gravity
the weight of stories
I feel
turn into starry nights
to heal.

messages from silent,
divine god humming.
creation is loud,
 I would hear
 the humming everyday.

life singing me alive,
this humming buzz.

~Constriction

Grapple.
your tenderness, delicious

then . . .

there is a criticism
this grappling force
you see in me —
daresay it's you?

Acceptance.
Can you trust in this heart I have?

I do.

Control I exude —
you scuba-sort the subtle waves.
I have not had to say
what I'm feeling.
It's becoming confusing
So we step away.

Ameliorate
this situation .
Let the situation be the teacher.

What of this is yours?
When to heal,
and when to be
 and let me be…
Be who I am,
with scars and stories.

We are clear. Pure at the core.

Let go of scrutiny,
 the scrupulous mind.
to allow
 feather-white
 love and light,
to shine.

Are you permeable?

We may collide with walls built tight
Non-porous fire dense
Can we let go of contraction and defense?
Let the electric light of our fires
Hum the radiant ballads through our blood.
Heart, eyes, fingertips...love.

~Am I Not, Not i

Pleasure
Body
Awake
Sense
Rivers
 Of tingling essence

Alive
I am
Am I not.
Not I.
Breath
Alive.

Offering this time
Birth unto life.
Again
And again.
All an offering
to be in body
shape size

fall away

pulsing sense

i am.
Am i not.
Not i
breath
alive.

Achievement
bows to moment.
dissolves
here.
drifts into birth
this breath
recognition of you
into me.
fine lines dissolve
grace parts ways.
to open space.
to melt and sway
drift into play

this may write
how it feels
to feel you:
first, body alive
and fresh joy
a baby in this time,
then a grasping
happening
when recalling
calls it in
and seeks its touch.

As if this is not enough.

Grace allows this all.

dependency dances
a pendulum swing,
and this is

alone again
all-one begin.
again.

Today
to write
feels like a
grapple
rappel
down
let images
appear
and form
lines
called words
verb
reverb.
play .

Sensation
memory
attach
detach
breathe
no worry.
breathe
offering.

breathe breath offering.

dance in This.
on the cliff
try, not try, to fall
let it happen
trying ceases
begins where it ends.
sudden life inject
full breath
yes
it can breathe into all THIS.

 Access the yes.
Before the no.
in open witness
newborn consciousness.
all allow
all-low, high
all is.

defense once
manifest
by eyelids
that was it.

we learn protection;
lines of separation
define deeper impressions
and mind creates
edges

all for,
the body tantra
to soften them.

edges
become

fibers
pliant with color
and dye-cast beauty.
Mind casts
smoothly
water over stone
fingers over strings.
play on the lines
and all that defines
this life
giving unto life.

definitions make love
in opposing rawness.
Life giving life
boundaries electrify
New life is realized.

play breathe
in heat,
grace breathe
burn,
melt vapor from warm water
it becomes One.

~Desire

Electric
timing. . .

our power is surmounting
again, words
are superfluous

to the super nova this is:

> bliss inside bliss
> outside to in,
> welcoming
> this into this.

You are art,
eye drafted for years
I crafted, to set aside fears

(Yes —that is a story tasting so sweet.)

As it all falls into alignment,
the work of my soul,
my true gifts now shine,
and I hold back no more.

Now I am ready to embody
what I always was and had to re-member
into cell walls and marrow.

Your unique heat
helps to engrave this embodied queen being.
My cup is full and with you,
 I'm not hungry.
Just ready.
 Open and present,
listening.

riding home, silent with grace,
desiring to support
and know what holds you,
in your challenges.

The silence I cultivate,
the lessons align.

simple no-mind.
with you,
I
return
home
to
me.

this love does not need Us
   ...to live
Nor we need it to live.
this Love Is.
It is.
Boundless,
   though found in the bounds.
Breathe it
   to free it.
It is free.
This breath is free.
This life living life is.
Living love is.

desire,
you are safe
to be free in me.
love loves you, dear desire.

Expand,
Free to feel,
fully feel,
fulfilled.

~Pu-erh tea , Purity

Pure this tea,
Steeping
Between you and me.
I am steeping.
You are stepping,
Away,
A slight step,
for a deep breath.

Sovereignty,
It is not glamorous.
It is the stark and raw
Biting glance of this,
This story still
Consuming me.
Feeding off . . .life energy..

Life returns,
As I face the story,
And lay it to rest
with bolts of
electric from my chest
heart, breast
calm and alive.
This.
Love.
This.
Waves of support
Resonate ajna, crown, and core.
Control is released.
Grace,
Relax,
Let it come.
All of this.

Rivers of light,
I relinquish rudders, to ride.

~Wings, as well

The healer's medicine,
The lover's dose
  Within.
He departs,
 Leaving
 leaping flames.

 I take flight again,
On my own wings,

(Embrace this little pear
  I invite him in,
   Bite into this,
   Delight in this,
   And share)

Still
 I'll leap off
This
Cliff,
Even if I don't have wings
That spread
Or arms
That catch.

The lover's arms
are wings, as well.

~We Suffuse

Trust, I trust.
The story unfolds,
each steeping stone
appears as I leap.
I keep leaping,
 licking
flames of light,
tickling
 exhales of air,
soft might,
might be, maybe,
yes,
I leapt up.

keeping up
leaping up
lets channel this
creative kiss
of sound and voice

aqueous
dance of body
in colliding
rhythmic study

Processing gives way
to the love of weight.

drape
onto me

to melt
we suffuse
heartbeats.

~Man, Goddess

Shakti shocking
 into the light.
We are so alive
 and tastes are bright.
Breathe through
 and purify.
Waters move by wind
emotions by breath.

My ego wants to know
That I teach you too…?

I may offer you
lemons
from my
Leaping
Loosened
Flames.

Let Leela loose
In me,
and she'll
Set free
your
Shakti shocking.

You say —

Many judge you,
Call you untouchable.
Fear speaks with haste.
I see through it.
Your love of life - I taste.

~We Spin Helical Dreams

mirrors make merry
   miracles,
in this sister kiss,
where in nothing is amiss
yet we still crave to taste it.

and our longing yields
to the presence of pain
and hopes already healed .. .
. . . .and healing,
through seeing me,
 seeing you.

I see grandma in you
and the mother too.
 Yet...
Sister envy stops ,
   catches a breath.

Grace.
I navigate
Your purgatory,
Shame and pain story,
I swim around it,
 Ripple empathy

Path ways
 give way
One wave
 to this wave.

Do we see, sister?

I'm on your side
 I dream weave your life with you.

 Your highest love,
 will shine and create,
Otherwise,
 how will any One elevate
 beyond the heart terrain,
  arranging from dis-ease?

I am you.
You are me.

There but for the grace of…
Is there for the grace of…
God go I,
 as I go for all.

Let us integrate
 with love, attention
 and ease
 the sick *and* sacred
  designs in holy tree-family.

Integrate for integrity,
 to unveil the truths
 our ancestors still breathe.

We breathe their evolution.

we spin helical dreams,
as our children breath in our ascendant genes.

~ the death

~Luscious Layers and Mundane Shades

I let go
 and let you go
So much so,
 the drama
and luscious
layers of fantasy
reveal raw reality.

I'm left with nothing,
 It ALL comes to me.

I recall.
Love is also the mundane:
The unexpected cloud shade
Falling moist into my
 glorious sunny summer.

accountability
has me counting no longer.

accountability from
the power of love
alive in nerve plexus
Of my hot summer sun
Above this womb
Fueling the room
Of a canyon heart space
Spacious. . .

gracious.

echoes fade to
create this...
  cry of the hawk,
  wings beat to glide
  drift on currents
    never to touch a horizon.
    because...

Horizons edge is an illusion
  on an eternal expanse,
Edge meets its match, Fear,
  the wise croaking elder,
    beckoning Edge closer.
She giggles in delight;

  Edge.
      never.
          arrives.

toes upon Edge's line,
  we are taught by Fear ...

to

fly.

Fly.

Fly?

Horizon forgotten
as memory fades
beyond mind,
landscape escapes.

~Where Breath Stops Cold

boundaries
built for
knowing me,
and
accounting for
the pain I conceived
upon that
immaculate conception

Soul,
north star,
direct my truth.
True is trust.
trust begets truth.
The truth of
soul needs
feels body-healthy.
Letting go
of immediacy
and gratification
of old needs.

New needs
new day,
this man,
this teacher,
this star bold friend.
He is a wizard,

a wild island.
Tea and chi,
mineral magic
makes alchemy

in my blood.

I'm talking
higher octave,
new need
8
steps
up.

I was
weeping for
forceps
that built force
into me,
from the first inhale
I could barely accept
this life rushing air
entering me.
In the waters
of between
I would have been pleased
to remain.

Alone, with myself,
nothing is hidden,

I feel where my breath
stops cold,
in the space just below
the throat,

near collarbone.

inhaling life
into here
is like ice cracking
the fear

of this life and its harsh
cold metals
and sterile hands,

midwifery hands
replaced
by the science of man,
I and so many
born without songs,
her sighs and moans,
born without
swift wisdom
and timeless medicine.

Years of running,
yields to feeling,
Body sinks,
to expose the root.

fear of letting life in.

Ice melts
life swells
in the space
of liquid release.
I am home here.
I am what I need.
I need nothing more.
as it is
 all
  always

here.

~Magicians, Muse-icians.

I am not your lover,
your sweetheart,
or lady.

I could own this,
 and you
by building a ship,
and in fact
I thought for a moon
that I did.

It bled out,
Yes I bled,
You dreamt,
womb wisps
 painted your bed.

It's all out now,
and we cannot deny
what truth wants to come through
and heal and soothe
our hearts open again
to the truth of our
knowing,
you hearing me,
and me seeing you.

hear the call
to be alone.

We collide,
to affirm it is the letting go
into being alone
that brings us close.

Offer
 hearts space.
breathe freedom
into the sails of this ship,
this friend ship
wherein
mystery
unfolds
and sounds
like glass harmonics
and timpani beats,
voices tremolo,
our voices in harmony.

So music was
 and is
the bridge.
No longer will
 I fight this.

Desire for union,
 all,
in a sacrum,
 so sacred.
It asks to be emptied,
 washed clear
 and aligned.
Shrine of desire,
6 octaves higher,
  make love
with your god heart.

Ethna's venus
is
 one
to make melodies spin
 love.

Star seeds are fertilized
and you're nesting into life.
Now is the time.
Sing paint produce and create.
Talk and teach less.
Listen and learn more.
 now.

Listen in the solitude
 and lean in close,

integrate truth,
instead of pain,
Integrity will ensue.

..which brings me to..

Is Ethna Venus ours?
She feels more like me,
a sovereign
 virgo queen.
I suppose I let you in,
with her iris green and
 crown of red,

a shared vision of creation.

You, dear friend,
 co-magician, musician
 muse.

Instigating, cooking
 teasing
my fertile being
into all
  I've always seen.

Penetration like this,
I have not felt before,
yet you're so familiar,
as though she was waiting,
for

 a wisdom
 allowed
 in. . .

to enter womb,
brush voice loom
with swift electric play,
remind me of life's Grace:

 she soars on smooth air
 and opens her voice
 to sing it all,
 coloring soundscapes.
 No more escape.
 into sex for
 safe's sake.
                this is a rare love,
                    made,
 when two
  create
  the child of songs and
 music magic that breaks
 spells and aches.

we Listen:
the sound of star fires
and moon pulling tide.

~Before You Can Shine

Before you can shine,
 you gotta burn.
Cast bronze;
 that's your loving work.
Trust this searing flame
 is not in vein.
Your heart is a wise welder.
 it knows
 pouring and time,
 flame and focus
 highly refined.

Trust.
Love.
Trust
you shine.

Blue and gold,
the blue flame knows
the seed
is a gem of
cool heat.

Blue and gold,
solar open throat.

~ the union

~Spirit Husband

Where are you now,
king of mine?

thick now,
growing into my muscle. . .

I had a dream of you, my love,
and I know you're walking on this earth,
I have smelled your scent
and your fingertips are calloused with her dirt.

Your shoulders they are hard and lean,
my head I rest upon your chest,
I want to feel you feeling me,
so, I surrender into the rest.

alluring and strong,
gentle and wise,
your arms come from behind
I acquiesce,

Safe.

There is great healing in creating,
painting in heart's re-arranging.
This mind is canvas stretched,
blank, open, smooth, un-etched.

To all that meets the need
of the true and healthy being,
my husband, my love,
my wild man with father hands,
let's ride this rapture
on wings of great measure,
through blue sky and flames,
through lazuli telepathy play,
til I'm ready to meet your face,
your chest,
hands and scent,
in this Earth shrine
  of embodiment.

With this wizard-kinda-witchy,
mundane and healing,
I pray to let go
of the ways I hold back,
of the need to call it something.
I pray to get out of the way,
to be more of
    the way.

This man of mythic designs
of my heart-dream,
it may be called destiny,
it is a working work of art,
a tender kind of coupling.
Gender melding equanimity.
Deep deep peace.

My spirit husband,
Wild eyed, solid, free –
  are you with me?

I surrender again
My belly Sun Ray

leads this way.

~Freedom

Return to childlike awe,
I agree to play with you.

I feel you,
my king.
I hear what you're asking
I listen more
 you become more
 of who you are
 In your own sovereign seat.
Sovereignty.
is the teacher
teaching,

 this womb pulse deep.

Story more than me,
my power,
or the primordial song
of women wounds.
 although -
a valid part and parcel
of this seeking,
healing humanity.

I listen; I hear…
The kings, fathers, brothers
channeling their power,
 we listen to each other

The pain bodies of gender
identifying and holding fast,
now surrender to the
burgeoning human union.
lines of confusion
diffusing in rebirth fusion.

Deep root, we be.
From sacral, we create
Through heart we breathe
and voice we weave
and our one eye bows

   we return to childlike awe.

~Shrine Designed

I could think
I have never known
a love
like this
before...

Yet, this love is a pattern,
 of a hum,
  of a strike,
   of two parts,
in my shrine-designed heart
 crafting more of this Life.
  to evolve and
   weave true equality

~Ride Emotion

Is my prayer
- my tastiest desire?
Sublimated,
 - with devotion,

into...
 silent steam curls
of

letting

go?

into...
...Elation as I fall
  into devotion,
  ride emotion,

Up

into the deep well?

Well...?

patience,
 my love, my child,
 be still.
there is a still
 we slowly build
 to distill.

evolution felt as involution,
more alive embodiment -
 this transcendence is.

~Home, Well, Home

Humbled I am,
each moment,
life-giving leaves
fall.

Clinging to what?
It is a ruthless fight
to prevent the wind-flight
that makes love to the wings
from whom I learned to sing.

Alone in this wood,
Layers reveal layers,
 I descend into the well
of this soul's inky mystery.

It is all,
   all over me.
I am all,
   all over it.

This wind, tree,
Golden rays
 silver streams
 of moon's robes,
Forever changing.

~Bones

Naiveté, I rub your spine,
  the well was just fine,
  all this time,
only needed breathing,
 tapping spring
  with pulsing navel,
    and springtime listening.

When your Dad left,
There were taxi cab ladies
and 2 am sofa sex,

Scared to be heard,
 you held our breath.

Held for years.

An orphan in heart,
you craved the handsome dark. . . .

        . . . a tuilerie
      seeks a marble pillar.

Now.

I dig up your bones,
hollow,
in the well...
I polish them off,
See them clearly,
honor their placement,
tracing their smooth cracks,
revealing constellations
of your night sky.

~The Door, You Walked Me To

I have fallen,
Again,
Again.
As I loosen my grip,
 it loosens its grip,
 belay is missed,

free climb
free fall.

I am humbled
Each day
as I break.

I break,
Yet not broken,
discover new softness.

Buoyant body of tenderness
 gentle self loving self.

I have gratitude
to give you,
- though you request
words less,
in accordance
to
that
morning dew,
perched on petals…

So I'll gather,
- then hand you -
the best of flora,
wet with this love
that I cannot conjure,
that I can only offer,
From the wellspring
waters of my deep being. . .

offering this:
. . . exquisite aloneness,

 visit me,
here, in. . .

a home, I built alone,
through the door, you walked me to.

~Discovery

home,

This womb,
This wholeness,
is a star family not broken,
a constellation connected
within my star seed womb.

home,

into love,
choosing this life.
into love,

being woman.

Patient and kind.
Stability deep within

The pelvis,
The cradle,
The home,
The womb.

~Celebration II

This fire,
Celestial
Celestite
Celebrates

Longing is the Be-Longing,
Coming home again
Again and again.

The fires have found home,
In the womb rising up
To cauldron
Of delicious desire fire
Into spirit steam
And ornate music poetry.

Dip paint
Thoughts in
 whirls wheels,
Brush dipped
 too much

The forgotten canvas waits,
this patient white space,
and breath of grace,
   waiting,
for pain to be paint
Swirled in ways
   of healing rapture
      and clearer mirrors.

~Vitality

there is devotion
you pour
into
vitality.

expansion
calculates.
I hear you articulate,
the webs your life pulse weaves.
 <<thank you>>
I have slowly opened
to receive.

I am silent
within the sound
of
a heart pulsing
summer thunder claps,
electric arcs,
of One love.
our beloved One.

we have been listening:
angel
breath
designs
and
aligns
our eyes,
more luminous
now,
and,
brimming
with nectar,
 our reflectors.
we share a still lake,
familiar warm water ,
rising up,
the
vapors from
this well,
heat in palms,
pressing upon

you,
 vast heart,
 boldly open.

still,
I remember,
the blossom opens. . . .
    . . . to open.